# The BLACK DEATH

EPIDEMIC!

# The BLACK DEATH

*by* STEPHANIE TRUE PETERS

**BENCHMARK BOOKS**

MARSHALL CAVENDISH
NEW YORK

# ACKNOWLEDGMENTS

With thanks to Sharon T. Strocchia, Associate Professor of History,
Emory University, Atlanta, Georgia, for her careful reading of the manuscript.

Benchmark Books
Marshall Cavendish
99 White Plains Road
Tarrytown, New York 10591-9001
www.marshallcavendish.com

Copyright © 2005 by Marshall Cavendish Corporation
Map copyright © 2005 by Mike Regan

Book design by Michael Nelson
Map by Mike Regan

LIBRARY OF CONGRESS CATALOGING-IN-PUBLICATION DATA
Peters, Stephanie True, 1965-
The Black Death / by Stephanie True Peters.
p. cm. — (Epidemic!)
Summary: Describes the 1347–1351 outbreak of plague in Europe, known as the Black Death,
which killed one out of three people and changed the course of European history.
Includes bibliographical references and index.
ISBN 0-7614-1633-1
1. Black Death—Europe—History—Juvenile literature. [1. Black Death.
2. Plague.] I. Title. II. Series.
RC178.A1P48 2003
362.1'9232'094—dc21
2003000743

Photo Research by Linda Sykes Picture Research, Hilton Head, SC

Photo credits: front cover: Musée d'Unterlinden, Colmar, France/Bridgeman Art Library; back cover: Prado,
Madrid/AKG, London; page v: British Library, London/AKG, London; pages vi and vii: Biblioteca Augusta Perugia/Dagli
Orti/The Art Archive; pages viii and ix, 28, 46: Musée Condé, Chantilly, France/Réunion des Musées Nationaux/Art
Resource, NY; page x: Hospital of Santa Maria Della Scala, Siena, Italy/AKG, London; page xi: Biblioteca Marciana,
Venice, Italy/Bridgeman Art Library; pages xiii, 4, 23, 30: AKG, London; pages 2, 10, 19, 32: Stock Montage; pages 3,
54, 56: Private Collection/Bridgeman Art Library; pages 9, 22: British Library, London/AKG, London;
11: British Library, London/Bridgeman Art Library; pages 12, 33: Bibliothèque Nationale, Paris/AKG, London;
15: Westfaelisches Schulmuseum, Germany/AKG, London; 20: Bibliothèque Royale, Brussels, Belgium/Visioars/AKG,
London; 31: University Library, Prague, Czech Republic/Giraudon/Art Resource, NY; 34: National Library, Brussels,
Belgium/AKG, London; 35: Bibliothèque Mazarine, Paris, France/Bridgeman Art Library; 39: Landesmuseum
Johanneum, Graz/AKG, London; 41: Biblioteca Laurenziana, Florence, Italy/Scala/Art Resource, NY; 43: Biblioteca di
San Marco, Venice/AKG, London; pages 44 and 45: Musée Condé, Chantilly/AKG, London; 48: Bradford Art Galleries
and Museums, West Yorkshire, UK/Bridgeman Art Library; 50: Galleria dell' Accademia/Rabatti-Domingie/AKG,
London; 52: The National Trust Photographic Library/Derrick Witty

PRINTED IN CHINA

135642

*Front cover: Suffering Man*, detail from the Isenheim Altarpiece by Matthias Grünewald, painted around 1510
*Back cover:* Detail from *Triumph of Death* by Pieter Brueghel the Elder, painted around 1560
*Half title:* 14th-century English manuscript illumination of a diseased woman with a bell to warn others of her infection
*Title Page:* 16th-century manuscript illumination of plague victims being cared for in Perugia, Italy
*From the Author, page vii:* A scene from a medieval hospital

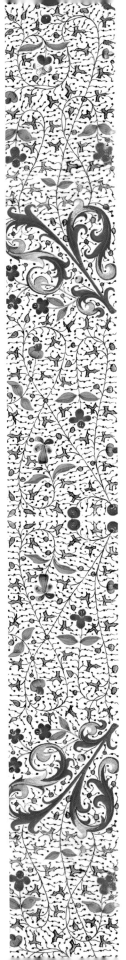

# CONTENTS

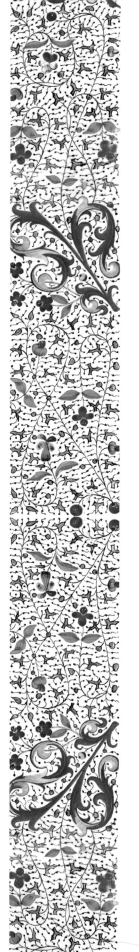

# FROM THE AUTHOR

The idea for a series of books about epidemics came to me while I was sitting in the doctor's office with my son. He had had a sleepless, feverish night. I suspected he had an ear infection and looked forward to the doctor confirming my diagnosis and prescribing antibiotics.

While waiting for the doctor to appear, I suddenly realized that the situation I was in—a mother looking to relieve her child's pain—was hardly new. Humans have had an ongoing battle against disease throughout history. Today we have tremendous knowledge of how the human body works. We understand how viruses and bacteria attack and how the body defends itself. Through immunizations and simple hygiene, we're often able to prevent disease in the first place. Our ancestors were not so knowledgeable, nor so lucky.

In this series I have tried to put a human face on five epidemics that laid millions low. All five occurred in the past and have since been medically controlled. Yet in some areas of the world, similar stories are still being played out today as humans struggle against such enemies as AIDS, Ebola virus, Hantavirus, and other highly contagious diseases. In the ongoing battle against disease, we may never have the upper hand. Microscopic foes are hard to fight.

Many survivors wrote of the horrors they witnessed; here, two travelers come face-to-face with a man covered with plague boils.

# ONE IN THREE

In the years from 1347 to 1351, one out of every three people in Europe died. Their deaths weren't the result of war. No earthquake or other natural disaster killed them. Their assailant was much more sinister. It attacked the body from within, silently and swiftly. The killer was the plague, later called the Black Death.

The cause of death was microscopic bacteria. The existence of such things was incomprehensible to people living in the Middle Ages. In fact, it would take more than five and a half centuries for the cause of the plague to be identified.

Much of what we know of these plague years comes from first-person accounts left by those who survived. Clerics, lawyers, writers, and others chronicled the daily scenes of death they saw unfold before them. Sometimes clinical and fact-filled, other times grief-stricken and appalled, these reports record the events and human responses to the horror.

The precise toll exacted by the plague can never be fully known. But its legacy was felt for decades afterward, when generations of survivors picked up the pieces of a shattered society and tried to put them back into some semblance of normal life.

# CHAPTER ONE

# *The* PLAGUE COMES ~ TO EUROPE ~

*In October 1347, at about the beginning of the month,*

*twelve Genoese galleys . . . put into the port of Messina. The Genoese carried such a*

*disease in their bodies that if anyone so much as spoke with one of them he was*

*infected with the deadly illness and could not avoid death.*

—*Michele da Piazza, Franciscan monk, ca. 1350*

THE BLACK DEATH entered the port city of Messina on the island of Sicily in October 1347. It traveled aboard trade ships en route from the East, where it had decimated populations. Now it would spread throughout Europe.

Medieval people blamed the plague on many things, including foul air, a glance from an infected person, and the wrath of God. But no one suspected that the real criminal was something much more tangible: the black rat.

The rat itself was not responsible for the disease. The true blame falls upon the bacteria that lived in the stomachs of the fleas that lived on the rats.

*Opposite:*

Merchant ships carried the plague into port cities.

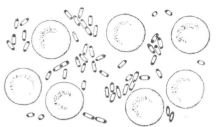

The rod shapes are the *Yersinia pestis* bacteria; the round shapes are blood corpuscles.

## THE PEST AND *Y. PESTIS*

The scientific name of the plague-causing bacterium is *Yersinia pestis*. *Y. pestis* is a rod-shaped bacterium that thrives within the stomach of the rat flea, *Xenopsylla cheopis*.

One *Y. pestis* can multiply into thousands in an hour. When the flea can no longer support the bacteria within its stomach, it disgorges them into the bloodstream of a host body as it bites the host and sucks its blood. The bacteria then infect the host, eventually killing it. Other fleas become infected when they suck the diseased host's blood. When they jump to a new host, they carry the disease with them.

Usually the flea's host is a small mammal such as the black rat. When the rat dies, the flea must find another host or perish. In the absence of other rats or small mammals, the flea can and will jump to a human.

Once infected, the human body soon begins to show signs of the disease. First fever, chills, nausea, and delirium set in. In the bubonic form of the plague, pus-filled swellings called buboes form in the neck, groin, and armpits. Dark spots appear on the skin, the result of bleeding beneath the skin's surface. A foul stench comes from the patient's body. His or her urine is thick and smelly. As the bacteria multiply, they infect the brain, lungs, and kidneys. The victim goes into shock or slips into a coma. Death occurs within three to six days of infection.

Before the age of antibiotics many, though not all, victims died from the bubonic form of the plague. Two other strains, the pneumonic and the septicemic, nearly always led to death—and much more quickly than the bubonic strain.

In the pneumonic plague, the bacteria, which are transmitted through the air, infect the lungs. In addition to fever, nausea, and delirium, the victim coughs up blood. With one sneeze, millions of plague-laden droplets are sent into the air. Anyone near enough to inhale these droplets can catch the disease. Death could occur within hours, though the patient can linger as long as three days. In the septicemic form, the bacteria infect the bloodstream after the victim is bitten by a flea. Death is all but assured within a day.

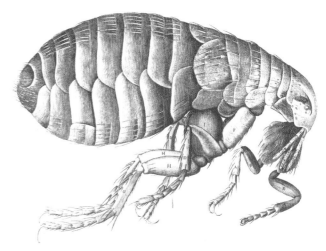

*Xenopsylla cheopis*, the rat flea, carrier of *Y. pestis*

Historians have argued about which strain of plague infected people during the Black Death years. First-person accounts of the symptoms point to a combination of the bubonic and pneumonic. Consider this description written in a letter by a musician from Avignon, France:

"People suffer an infection of the lungs . . . [and] die within two days. . . . It is the most contagious, for when one infected person dies everyone who saw him during his illness . . . immediately follows him. . . . There is another form of the disease that exists alongside the first one, in which boils erupt suddenly in the armpits."

The seasons during which the plague struck also seem to indicate both the bubonic and pneumonic forms. In the winter, when fleas are dormant, the bubonic form died down. When spring arrived and fleas became active again, bubonic plague attacks began anew. The pneumonic strain, being transmitted through airborne particles, was around throughout the year.

Whichever form it was, there is no doubt that the plague found its victims by the hundreds, then the thousands, and finally the millions. It swept from one region to the next, staying for four to six months before running its course.

# WERE MEDIEVAL PEOPLE REALLY PLAGUED ⟨⟩ WITH THE PLAGUE? ⟨⟩

There have been recent discussions among some historians as to whether the medieval epidemic was actually the plague. These historians base their arguments on different interpretations of evidence taken from primary source material.

Some historians point to the fact that nowhere in this material is there any suggestion of an epizootic of rats. *Epizootic* is the term used to describe a disease that kills a huge number of a particular animal. For years it's been accepted that humans became infected with the bubonic plague because the black rat population died, leaving the fleas no alternative but to turn to humans for a meal. Thus the death of the rat population could have served as an omen of the epidemic that followed.

Yet there is no mention of a large number of dead rats anywhere in the documents that remain from the Middle Ages. Why not? Perhaps, some say, it's because dead rats were so much a part of everyday medieval life that a greater number of bodies was hardly worth noticing.

But other scholars speculate that the reason dead rats aren't mentioned is that the disease was not, in fact, the plague. They claim the symptoms described by medieval writers can be inter-

preted as any number of other illnesses, including tuberculosis, anthrax, and typhoid.

Still others maintain that it was the plague, but not the plague as we know it today. They suggest that the *Y. pestis* bacterium we're familiar with had a different, perhaps more virulent form in the Middle Ages, which is why it struck with such deadly force. Modern medical researchers have long been aware that bacteria and viruses mutate, often becoming stronger and immune to medication. This fact is one of the reasons the AIDS virus has been so hard to combat. And the medical profession has recently warned that the overuse of antibiotics—drugs that kill bacteria—is leading to a critical situation. Soon, they say, bacteria could become immune to the antibiotics, making the drugs worthless even as the bacteria grow in strength.

Their warnings seem to be worth listening to. In Madagascar, a new, virulent form of the plague has struck that is resistant to the antibiotics.

We may never know the absolute truth about the epidemic of the Middle Ages. The bodies of the dead are long since gone. We only have the words of their contemporaries to guide us, and those words seem to point most conclusively to the plague.

## "THE ENTIRE INHABITED WORLD CHANGED"

Medieval Europe was not the first region devastated by the plague. In 1346 reports were heard of a dread disease killing thousands in the Orient and the Middle East.

The Orient was easy prey. From roughly 1333 to 1345, China suffered from a series of catastrophes. Drought parched the land, making it nearly impossible to keep crops alive. Floods followed the drought, and soon famine threatened the country. Earthquakes destroyed villages. Swarms of locusts ravaged the countryside, devouring the remaining vegetation and leaving a hungry people even hungrier. Then the plague settled in.

By the end of 1346, the Chinese population had been ravaged by the disease. Meanwhile the plague traveled along trade routes westward into the Islamic world. An Arab historian named Ibn-Khaldūn knew of the plague's horrors firsthand: his own parents died from it. He wrote:

"Civilization both in the East and the West was visited by a destructive plague, which devastated nations and caused populations to vanish. It swallowed up many of the good things of civilization and wiped them out. . . . Cities and buildings were laid waste, roads and way signs were obliterated, settlements and mansions became empty and dynasties and tribes grew weak. The entire inhabited world changed."

In less than a year, that "inhabited world" would include Europe.

## THE PLAGUE'S JOURNEY FROM EAST TO WEST

Two traditional stories survive that tell how the disease may have been transmitted from East to West. The first, mentioned earlier, is that of the twelve diseased ships that docked at Messina, Sicily, in October 1347.

When the citizens of Messina realized they were under attack from a highly contagious disease, many fled the town. Some went to nearby Catania to seek shelter and aid. Neither the Catanians nor the Messinans realized the Messinans were carrying the disease with them. The Catanians welcomed them into their walled city. Then the Catanians began to fall ill as well. The plague overwhelmed their city as it had Messina. From there it slowly spread.

Sicily was overcome within a few months. Sicilians fled to the Italian mainland, bringing the plague with them. Death took up residence wherever they did.

The second story of how the plague reached Europe places the point of contact in Kaffa (now called Feodosiya) in the Crimea. Kaffa was a Genoese trading colony on the northern shores of the Black Sea. In 1346 violence erupted between the Christian Genoese and the Muslim Turks, known as Tatars. The Genoese retreated to safety inside Kaffa's high walls.

The Tatars laid siege to the colony. The only means of escape for the Genoese was aboard a nearby fleet of ships. However, slipping past the Tatars and reaching those ships seemed impossible.

Then the Tatars began to die of a horrible disease.

Gabriele de Mussis, an Italian lawyer and chronicler from Piacenza, lived through the plague in Italy. Though not an actual eyewitness to the events in Kaffa, he recounted the accepted story of how the Tatars tried to win the battle against the Genoese:

"They ordered corpses to be placed in catapults and lobbed into the city in the hope that the intolerable stench would kill everyone inside. What seemed like mountains of dead were thrown into the city. . . . Soon the rotting corpses tainted the air and poisoned the water supply."

The Genoese dumped body after body into the sea. But in the end, they opted to make a run for it. They succeeded in reaching their ships and sailed away from death.

Or so they thought. Either contact with the dead Tatars or the diseased rats that had infiltrated Kaffa had infected the Genoese. As the ships approached Italy in January 1348, those on board began to die of the same disease that had killed the Tatars.

Venice and Genoa were the first ports the doomed ships reached. Believing that the ships brought with them wonderful treasures and important goods from faraway lands, the residents of these cities welcomed them openly.

De Mussis describes what happened next:

"Alas, once our ships had brought us to port we went to our homes. . . . Relations, kinsmen, and neighbors flock[ed] to us from all sides. But, to our anguish, we were carrying the darts of death. While they hugged and kissed us we were spreading poison from our lips."

The citizens realized too late that those aboard ship were diseased. The plague had made landfall. Within months the trade routes throughout Europe acted as superhighways for the disease. Every place touched by a plague ship or caravan— Pisa, Genoa, Venice, Marseilles, Barcelona—was infected. Once a region was infected, nothing could help it.

# CHAPTER TWO

# EUROPE BEFORE
## ~ THE PLAGUE ~

*The one who was poorly nourished by insubstantial food fell victim to the merest*

*breath of the disease; the impoverished crowd of common folk*

*died a welcome death, since for them life was death.*

—Simon de Couvin, French chronicler, ca. 1350

**W**HAT WAS LIFE LIKE IN EUROPE when the plague struck? In 1347 Europe was in an era of urbanization. However, the agrarian-based economy and society that had developed at the collapse of the Roman Empire was still the main way of life.

When the Roman Empire fell in the fifth century, Europe underwent a period of chaos. Political power that had once been wielded by a sole Roman emperor was now broken up among warring nobles. Trade across the Mediterranean all but vanished. Cities and towns dependent on that trade shriveled and died.

People slowly migrated to the countryside to seek a living. Land became the primary source of wealth. In many parts of

Europe, society was divided into two groups: those who owned land, the nobles, and those who worked the land, the peasants. The relationship between these two groups became known as manorialism, so named because it revolved around the manor.

Hardworking peasants harvest grain under the watchful eye of their lord's overseer.

## MANOR LIFE

The manorial community consisted of the manor house, where the lord and his family lived; the lord's fields, orchards, forests, and ponds; plus a village with a church, a mill, and sometimes a wine press. Peasants lived in simple cottages in the village.

Without money or land of their own, most peasants were serfs; although not slaves, they were tied to the land in servitude to their lord. In exchange they were given a place to live, land to farm, and protection from enemies.

The manor house and outbuildings were often surrounded by strong fortifications.

A typical peasant dwelling had one or two rooms with clay and wood walls, a thatched roof, and hard-packed dirt flooring, sometimes strewn with straw. In the early Middle Ages, windows were simple openings, although in the later centuries they were usually covered with cloth. Fireplaces underwent change, too, from an open circle in the middle of the main room to a stone hearth set off to one side, with a chimney to vent the smoke.

Peasants lived with filth—their own, their animals', and that made by the simple act of living. Bathing was considered harmful. Garbage was thrown into the roads outside of the houses. Human waste accumulated in private areas close to the dwellings.

Lice, fleas, ticks, and rodents thrived in these conditions. They took up residence in hair, on skin, in the walls, roofs, and floors of the buildings. People had no choice but to live with them.

While the lord and his family enjoyed greater advantages than the peasants, they were not immune to some of the same problems that befell the poor. If the crops failed, the noble family felt the scarcity of food—though not as much as peasants, of course. The nobles were plagued by vermin because they shared the peasants' disregard for personal hygiene. Diseases transmitted by these vermin were just as likely to infect a noble as a peasant.

Nobles were often as ignorant and illiterate as the people they ruled. In fact, just about the only people who knew how to read and write were members of the clergy, a very powerful segment of medieval society.

In country villages livestock lived in the house. They helped keep peasants warm but sometimes were the source of disease.

## THE CHURCH

Although medieval Europe was divided into many small political entities, it was united by religion. Medieval people saw the hand of God in all things and believed in and were taught to follow the teachings of the Bible. In the Middle Ages you belonged to the Catholic Church unless you were among the small minority of people who were Jewish or who were members of some other non-Christian faith.

The Catholic Church had a strict hierarchy. At the top was the pope. Beneath him were the archbishops. Each archbishop was in charge of an archdiocese. An archdiocese was made up

A monk at work in a room in his monastery. Monasteries, communities of men devoted to God and the Church, safeguarded much of the written knowledge of the era.

of several dioceses, each headed by a bishop. Each diocese was in turn made up of parishes. It was in the churches of these parishes that people came to worship.

Abbots, monks, and village priests were vital in spreading the word of God to the people. No manor was without a village priest or access to a nearby monastery. Through these individuals and institutions, the Church reached every Christian in Europe.

The village priest had many duties in addition to his weekly sermons. He gave last rites to the dying, buried the dead, and performed marriages and baptisms. He heard confessions and gave absolution. He offered prayers and, sometimes, practical aid in times of sickness and suffering. Often the only literate person on the manor, he was sometimes the lord's secretary.

The Church was the wealthiest landowner in Europe. The noble class was expected to provide for the daily needs of monks and clergy. They did so by endowing lands to the Church. The Church ran these lands much as a noble would run his, with serf labor or monks of lower birth to work the fields.

Few people begrudged the Church its wealth. They believed that so long as the Church stood strong and offered guidance, they were protected by God.

## THE REBIRTH OF THE TOWN

For nearly five centuries after the fall of Rome, little happened to alter how life was lived. Then, from 950 to 1250, things changed—slowly, but dramatically. The population of Europe boomed—from 25 million to 75 million people. Several factors caused this explosion.

First, wide-scale invasion and war were on the decline, so fewer men were dying on the points of spears and swords. More men meant more families with children and more laborers to work the land.

Second, agricultural innovations such as improved plows and harnesses, the use of water mills and windmills, and a better understanding of crop rotation helped farmers get greater yields out of their fields. Forests were cut down and swamps drained to provide additional farmland. More food meant healthier people who produced children who lived past infancy.

Third, the weather underwent a general warming trend, giving even northern areas milder winters and drier summers. Milder winters meant fewer people died of cold and illness. Crop yields improved during the drier summers.

And fourth, there was no occurrence of a killer epidemic.

As the population increased, the traditional manor could no longer support all who had a claim on it. These people needed someplace to go and some means with which to support themselves. They turned to towns.

Towns had started to develop before the population explosion. In the ninth century, walled communities were built for protection against invaders. Markets often cropped up around monasteries, cathedrals, and, later, universities. Peasants with surplus produce or wares to sell could set up a brisk trade near or within such places. From these early beginnings, towns developed. By the mid-thirteenth century, some towns had swelled into cities. London, Paris, and Florence boasted populations of fifty thousand people and more. The population explosion was not, however, the only reason for the development of urban centers: Trade and commerce had been reborn.

After the fall of Rome, trade between the East and the West had greatly fallen off. Then, starting in the eleventh century, old trade routes began to reopen. This reopening was due in large part to the Crusades, religious wars fought between Christians and Muslims from 1095 to 1291. In 1095 Christian nobles were called upon by the pope to journey overland to the Holy Land to fight for religious supremacy and to acquire lands. Although the Crusades proved ineffectual for the Europeans in gaining lasting control over Muslim lands, the wars did help reestablish connections between the East and the West. These connections reopened old trade routes—along which the Black Death would make its terrifying way.

## LIFE IN THE TOWNS

What was a town like? Because towns were not planned, they had a haphazard layout. Surrounding the whole was a protective wall with two or more main gated entrances. Some people lived outside the wall but, in the face of an attack, everyone could hole up inside, relatively safe from harm.

Just inside the main gate was the bustling marketplace. Every day but Sunday, merchants, farmers, and artisans would hawk their goods. Side by side with the merchants' stalls were traveling musicians and jugglers who performed before crowds for money. Colorful tents and banners added to the carnival atmosphere of the marketplace.

Beyond the marketplace were the streets and buildings that

*Opposite:*
Lively marketplaces were the main attraction in many medieval towns.

made up the residential community. Buildings often rose several stories because space within the town's walls was limited.

Towns grew ever more crowded as people moved from the country. Houses were packed close together. The poorest people lived in single-floor thatch-roofed huts overshadowed by the bigger dwellings of the prosperous merchants. The richest people lived in large mansions set as far away from the thatched huts as possible. Most buildings doubled as places of business. A craftsman or merchant might run his business out of the front or first floor of his house and live in the back or upper stories.

Space for animals was limited. Cows and horses were usually stabled, but pigs, dogs, and chickens roamed the streets virtually unchecked. In the winter they lived with their owners.

Although the main marketplace streets were fairly wide and sometimes paved with cobblestones, the back streets were cramped, dimly lit, and made of hard-packed earth. Raw sewage ran down gutters on the side or in the middle of the streets. Manure was piled outside the stable entrances. Garbage rotted everywhere. The stench and filth could be overwhelming.

Flies, rodents, and other vermin flourished in such conditions. So did infectious diseases. Intestinal ailments, respiratory infections, and such horrifying conditions as leprosy spread easily in the crowded, unsanitary conditions of towns. But no disease spread as quickly or killed as many as that which was soon to strike.

## 1347: THE STAGE IS SET FOR PLAGUE
The twelfth, thirteenth, and early fourteenth centuries were times of economic and social growth in Europe. Prosperity

brought a lighthearted, almost optimistic mood. Then, at the start of the fourteenth century, things changed.

Weather conditions turned cold and wet. Crops rotted in flooded fields. Early snows and late frosts killed buds on fruit trees.

More land was being farmed, but it was often not as fertile as established fields. This, combined with the inclement weather, led to consecutive years of crop failure. And to top it off, cattle and sheep were stricken with murrain, a deadly infection. Meat, milk, wool, and leather became scarce.

Natural and man-made disasters shook Europe as well. Earthquakes reduced parts of Italy to rubble. Floods washed away roads and made travel nearly impossible. War broke out between England and France that lasted for generations (it became known as the Hundred Years War).

Less food. More people. Civil chaos. All these factors added up to famine. Malnourished and weak, people were more prone to sickness.

Rodents, on the other hand, flourished. When the forests were cut down for farmland, fuel, and building material, rats and mice were forced from their homes. They took up residence in the thatched roofs, straw floor coverings, and wood and mud walls of the typical home, bringing with them disease-carrying lice and fleas.

The very fact that people were so used to having pests about may have made them unaware when a new type of rodent moved into their towns.

# CHAPTER THREE

# EYEWITNESSES TO
## ~ DEATH ~

*How many gallant gentlemen, fair ladies, and sprightly youths . . .*
*having breakfasted in the morning with their kinsfolk, acquaintances and friends,*
*supped that same evening with their ancestors in the next world!*
—Giovanni Boccaccio, The Decameron

Y 1348 EUROPE LAY BESIEGED BY THE PLAGUE. No region was spared. City, town, country manor, monastery, village—all fell victim eventually.

Some people who lived through the plague years documented what they saw and heard. Their reports offer a glimpse of the devastation witnessed in different countries. The details paint scenes that are gruesome, tragic, and macabre.

## ITALY

Italian author Giovanni Boccaccio (1313–1375) left one of the best known accounts of the plague in his book *The Decameron*, a tale about ten young people who flee the city of Florence to escape the plague. The introduction contains vivid descriptions of the disease. One of the most telling passages reveals the depths of the people's fear:

"This scourge had implanted so great a terror in the hearts of men and women that brothers abandoned brothers, uncles their nephews, sisters their brothers, and in many cases wives deserted their husbands. But even worse, and almost incredible, was the fact that fathers and mothers refused to nurse and assist their own children, as though they did not belong to them."

The disease struck young and old, rich and poor. The rich at least had some comfort in knowing that if they paid enough money to the right people, they would be nursed until their deaths and their corpses would be buried in the cemetery of their choice. The poor, on the other hand, suffered without comfort. Boccaccio described their plight:

"Being confined to their own parts of the city, they fell ill daily in their thousands, and since they had no one to assist

Wealthy Italians attend the burial of plague victims.

them or attend to their needs, they inevitably perished almost without exception. Many dropped dead in the open streets, both by day and by night, whilst a great many others, though dying in their own houses, drew their neighbors' attention to the fact more by the smell of their rotting corpses than by any other means. And what with these, and the others who were dying all over the city, bodies were here, there and everywhere."

The scene in Florence was played out elsewhere in Italy. Chronicler Agnolo di Tura del Grasso (ca. 1300—1351) of Siena left this account:

"Members of a household brought their dead to a ditch as best they could, without priest, without divine offices. . . . All were thrown in those ditches and covered over with earth. And as soon as those ditches were filled more were dug. And I . . . buried my five children with my own hands."

Del Grasso intersperses numbers of dead with horrified observations of dogs pulling corpses from graves and wolves feasting on bodies in the countryside. His anguish comes through simply but with great strength in one line in particular:

"And it was all so horrible that I, the writer, cannot think of it and so will not continue."

Del Grasso also bemoaned the fact that when the plague struck, Siena had to abandon building a new cathedral. Too many of the workers had died. Construction on the cathedral was finally finished in 1464.

As Italy slowly succumbed, certain measures, in some cases very dramatic, were taken to try to prevent the disease— or, when it was clear the plague could not be stopped, to keep it contained.

The best way of preventing the plague was to make sure the infection didn't reach a city in the first place. Ships were turned away from coastal cities. Emigration from and visits to infected areas were forbidden. Goods and foodstuffs from outside areas were carefully monitored, if allowed into the city at all.

Inevitably, however, the plague did penetrate the city walls. Then it was a matter of keeping the plague's spread to a minimum.

In Pistoia, only members of a dead person's family could attend the funeral. The city of Venice ordered all dead to be buried at remote sites in graves at least five feet deep. Milan laid down the most dramatic and unsympathetic regulation: the city ordered any home with plague victims to be boarded up—with the sick *and* the healthy inside. Such a measure all but assured the death of the inhabitants. As inhumane as the regulation was, when the plague was over, Milan's death rate turned out to be one of the lowest in Italy.

Italy's major cities gasped for breath beneath the mountains of dead. By the end of 1348, the plague had done its worst and seemed to be subsiding. However, other countries in southern Europe were still reeling from the plague's impact.

# GO FIGURE

First-person accounts of the plague often include numbers of dead for the city about which the chronicler is writing. But how accurate are those numbers?

Careful searches through a variety of historic records, such as death records kept by the Church and lists of annual heriots (payments made upon the death of a serf by the serf's family), show that some figures were inflated. This may have been done either for dramatic purposes or because the author was so overwhelmed by the continual procession of dead bodies that a lesser number seemed inaccurate. Take, for instance, Giovanni Boccaccio's reckoning that "over one hundred thousand human lives were extinguished within the walls of the city of Florence." Since Florence only had 100,000 "human lives" in 1347, this figure was clearly exaggerated for effect.

Likewise, the death rate in Avignon, France, was put at between 62,000 and 120,000, yet only 50,000 people were reckoned to live in that city at the time. Pope Clement VI listed the number of dead in Asia, India, and the Middle East as 23,840,000, but it seems unlikely that this figure was based on any real accounting. Instead, the very hugeness of the figure was meant to strike awe into Europeans just starting to be hit by the plague themselves.

Other figures, however, seem based on fact. The best records of death were kept by monasteries. The numbers there show just how hard these closed communities were hit. The Dominican monastery of Montpellier in southern France housed 140 souls; all but seven died of the plague. Gherardo, brother of the Italian poet Petrarch, was the sole survivor of his Carthusian monastery, save for his dog. He buried 34 monks.

Noble families also kept records of deaths, often leaving them with their church along with a chantry, an endowment paid so that the church would include the dead in its prayers during masses. From these records we can see how certain families were nearly wiped out during the plague.

Careful sifting through the fact and fiction of records leads historians to the conclusion that one-third of the population of Europe perished during the Black Death—25 million people, a staggering number in anyone's book.

## FRANCE

The plague reached France in January 1348. Marseilles, a port city on the southern coast of France, was struck first. From there the disease traveled inland along established trade routes. It reached Paris by summer and swept through the rest of the country by the year's end.

Paris was the home of the Hôtel de Dieu, the most sophisticated medieval medical hospital. Run by the Church, the Hôtel de Dieu was not a place where people came to be cured, but rather to be cared for and kept isolated so that others might not catch their disease. In short, it was a place to die.

Jean de Venette (d. 1369), abbot of the Carmelite monastery in Paris, gives a description of the Hôtel de Dieu during the height of the plague. In one notable passage he offers high praise for the dedication of the nuns attending the sick:

"So high was the mortality at the Hotel-Dieu in Paris that for a long time, more than five hundred dead were carried

A plague victim is carried into the Hôtel de Dieu, where nuns will care for him.

*Opposite:* Infected monks are blessed by a priest.

daily with great devotion in carts to the cemetery of the Holy Innocents in Paris for burial. A very great number of the saintly sisters of the Hotel-Dieu who, not fearing to die, nursed the sick in all sweetness and humility, with no thought of honor . . . rest in peace with Christ."

As the disease swept through France, panic-stricken people abandoned all semblance of humanity. In a letter to Cardinal Giovanni Colonna, a musician from the town of Avignon wrote:

"The sick are treated like dogs by their families—they put food and drink next to the sick bed and then flee the house. . . . Neither kinsmen nor friends visit the sick. Priests do not hear the confessions of the sick, or administer the sacraments to them."

## NORTHERN EUROPE

Northern Europe soon succumbed just as southern Europe had. Gilles li Muisis, abbot of Saint Giles at Tournai, a city in what is now Belgium, recounted what he saw in his town:

"Every day the bodies of the dead were borne to the churches: now five, now ten, now fifteen. And in the church of St. Brice, sometimes twenty or thirty. And in all parishes the priests, parish clerks and grave diggers earned their fees by tolling the passing bells by day and night, in the morning and in the evening; and thus everyone in the city, men and women alike, began to be afraid."

Fear was everywhere throughout Europe, but in some places people tried to counteract it, as this excerpt from a chronicle written in a monastery in Austria shows:

"Thoughtful men resolved that they should try to cheer each other up with comfort and merrymaking, so that they were not overwhelmed by depression. Accordingly wherever they could they held parties and weddings with a cheerful heart, so that by rekindling a sort of half-happiness they could avoid despair."

## ENGLAND, IRELAND, AND SCOTLAND

While the plague raged in continental Europe, England remained in good health, thanks in large part to the barrier provided by the English Channel. But then, "in 1348, about the feast of St. Peter in chains [1 August] the first pestilence arrived in England at Bristol, carried by merchants and sailors."

The plague made its way from port to port and town to town with traders and travelers, killing with as much ferocity as it had elsewhere in Europe. A monk from Yorkshire, Thomas Burton, wrote:

"The pestilence held such sway in England at that time that there were hardly enough people left alive to bury the dead, or enough burial grounds to hold them. . . . The pestilence grew so strong that men and women dropped dead while walking in the streets, and in innumerable households and many villages not one person was left alive."

Another monk, John Clynn of Kilkenny, Ireland, recorded his belief that he and the rest of humanity would soon be dead of the plague. He seems more concerned for his chronicle than for his own life:

"I, seeing these many ills, and that the whole world is encompassed by evil, waiting among the dead for death to come, have committed to writing what I have truly heard and examined; and so that the writing does not perish with the writer . . . I leave parchment for continuing the work, in case anyone should still be alive in the future and any son of Adam can escape this pestilence and continue the work thus begun."

Scotland as well as Ireland was laid low by the plague. Geoffrey le Baker, an English clerk, recalls somewhat triumphantly how the Scots fell ill soon after they had mocked the weakened English:

"With such a disaster laying England waste, the Scots gleefully swore that they would beat the English. They used to swear this jokingly (and blasphemously) 'by the foul death of the English'. But their joy was replaced by grief. The sword of the wrath of God, withdrawn from the English, punished the Scots."

The records left behind in Europe tell a vivid story. Bodies piled in streets. Corpses stacked like wood in huge pit graves. Towns and manors deserted but for skeletal remains. Families torn apart by grief, abandonment, and death. Fields in ruin and animals left unattended, wandering through countryside and city streets.

And throughout it all, people asked the same unanswerable question: Why?

# CHAPTER FOUR

# WHERE DID IT
## ⚚ COME FROM? ⚚

*[God said] let the planets poison the air and corrupt the whole earth; let there be universal grief and lamentation. Let the sharp arrows of sudden death have dominion throughout the world. Let no one be spared.*
—Gabriele de Mussis, medieval lawyer and chronicler

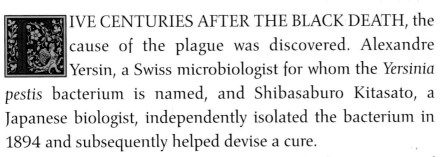

IVE CENTURIES AFTER THE BLACK DEATH, the cause of the plague was discovered. Alexandre Yersin, a Swiss microbiologist for whom the *Yersinia pestis* bacterium is named, and Shibasaburo Kitasato, a Japanese biologist, independently isolated the bacterium in 1894 and subsequently helped devise a cure.

But people living in the Middle Ages had no concept of microbiology or bacteria. In the minds of many, God had sent the dreadful disease as punishment for sin.

## GOD AND THE HEAVENS
What sins had they committed that deserved such retribution?

Two men pray for deliverance from the pestilence.

Some were sure the answers lay in the immoral behavior of their neighbors. Others were convinced that laziness and dishonesty were the root of the evil. Still others claimed that God was angry because they hadn't worshiped properly.

Frantic to save themselves, people flocked to the cathedrals and churches. They prayed for forgiveness, confessed their sins, and took communion. Others walked the streets dressed in rags and covered with ashes in an attempt to appear humble and penitent before God. Still others went on pilgrimages to holy sites, touched the bones and other relics of saints, and raised statues and shrines to the Virgin Mary and the saints associated with healing and disease.

Yet people still died, the virtuous and immoral, rich and poor, young and old. Nothing anyone did to appease God seemed to work.

## THE MIASMA THEORY

Most people felt sure they knew *why* God had sent the disease. Many also believed they knew *how* God sent it, and how the disease spread.

In the Middle Ages the "science" of astrology was very closely tied with religion. God controlled the movements of the planets, sun, moon, and stars. How He chose to arrange the heavenly bodies affected life—and death—on earth. Earthquakes, floods, drought, and other natural disasters therefore had supernatural causes.

The medical profession subscribed to this belief. In fact, a report made by the medical faculty of the University of Paris, one of the greatest medical communities of the Middle Ages, had little to do with practical medicine or knowledge of the human body. It stated there had been an unusual confluence of Mars, Saturn, and Jupiter in the House of Aquarius on March 20, 1345, at 1:00 P.M. This astrological occurrence, they said, had led to the epidemic now at hand.

Jupiter, a warm and humid body, had drawn noxious vapors into the air. Hot and dry Mars had ignited the vapors into a poisonous cloud, or miasma, that originated near India. Wherever the cloud drifted, the pestilence landed. Disaster and death, as predicted by the positions of Jupiter and Saturn, followed the cloud.

Though few debated the presence of the cloud, not everybody agreed with the faculty's findings. Some believed that the miasma had originated in China, where great earthquakes had broken open the land and released toxic fumes. Others had heard tales of strange storms and of sheets of fire burning whole cities. One story claimed the miasma was caused by the poisonous stench of dead fish that had been killed when the seas evaporated during a battle between the sun and the stars.

## THE PLAGUE MAIDEN
Many medieval people also believed in the existence of supernatural beings. One story of how the plague spread told of a beautiful witch called the Plague or Pest Maiden. The maiden

was "born" as a blue flame from the mouth of a dying patient. She carried a red scarf and flew from house to house. When she waved the scarf through an open window or door, those within fell victim. According to legend, the plague was stopped in one Austrian village when a brave man chopped off the maiden's scarf-holding hand.

## THE MEDICAL VIEW

In later years doctors wore beaked masks filled with flowers and spices to protect them from deadly smells.

Along with the miasma theory, doctors had other ideas of how the disease spread. Many believed that the smell from a dying plague victim could lead to infection—not surprising, since the stench from an unwashed body festering with oozing buboes was sickening. Although the smell wasn't to blame, the doctors were correct in thinking something in the air caused the plague—pneumonic plague is, after all, transmitted by airborne bacteria.

To counteract the smell and to prevent infection from the poisonous plague cloud, people carried nosegays or sacks of spices. Many doctors recommended filling a house with smoke. Green wood and aromatic branches and leaves made a great deal of smoke when burned and were therefore considered the most effective. Rosemary, camphor, and even sulfur were sometimes burned, too, giving homes a rich, rank odor thought sure to drive out the miasma.

Though smoke didn't directly cure the plague, the advice to burn fires may have saved at least one person. Guy de Chauliac, the most prominent physician of the day, advised Pope Clement VI to sit between two burning fires. The pope survived the plague, although probably because the fires kept fleas from his body—and possibly because he isolated himself from the sick.

Many people, including doctors, were convinced that a mere look or touch from a plague victim could kill. Even coming into contact with a patient's clothes or blankets meant chancing infection. These ideas were not so far-fetched, given that a cough from a pneumonic plague patient or fleas in clothing and blankets could transmit the disease.

But the medical community was far from understanding why such coughs and contact could lead to death. Physicians were also far from being able to treat the plague with any real cure. Many refused to even try. Others, however, did what they could to help cure patients.

Medieval medicine was based on a belief in the body's four "humors": phlegm, blood, yellow bile, and black bile. These humors had particular properties. Phlegm was cold and wet. Blood was hot and wet. Yellow bile was hot and dry. Black bile was cold and dry.

When a person was sick, his or her humors were considered out of balance. Curing a patient meant bringing those humors back into balance. In the case of

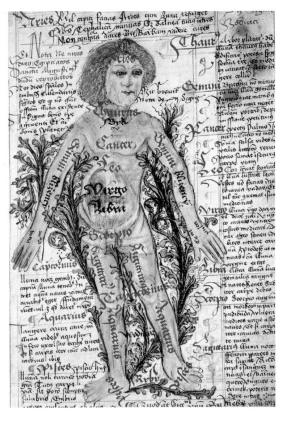

A page from a medieval medical book. Doctors believed the influence of heavenly bodies caused particular illnesses.

Bloodletting *(left)* was a common treatment for many ailments, including plague.

the plague, it was believed that the body had too much blood; therefore, bleeding a victim of excess blood would restore health.

Bleeding was thought to have other virtues, too. Most doctors believed the plague spread through the body via blood vessels. Redirecting the blood out of the body before it reached a major organ kept it from being affected by the plague's poison.

After consulting the astrologic signs of the day (or not, depending on how much the patient could pay or how much time the doctor wanted to spend near the patient), the doctor chose a specific spot to cut. The goal was to stop the bleeding just before the patient fainted—though it was a skilled doctor who could accurately predict when that moment would occur.

Other doctors subscribed to the school that said "like follows like." The idea was to draw the plague poison out of a body by applying a foul concoction to an obviously affected part of the body such as a bubo. Doctors lanced the pus-filled swellings, then laid any one of an assortment of mixtures on the oozing sore. Some of the more outlandish recipes included such ingredients as dried human feces and dried toads.

Not all doctors took such extreme measures. Some prescribed something much simpler: a lighter diet, optimistic frame of mind, prayer, and abstinence from sex. Another recommendation was not to bathe, since bathing opened pores, giving air poisoned with plague a doorway into the body. Some warned against sleeping on one's back because it allowed the noxious vapors free access to the nostrils.

# ☙ STAY THE HAND OF DEATH ☙

As the Black Death swept through Europe, people turned to magic, to medicine, and to prayer in the hopes of warding off death.

The word *abracadabra* was thought to be particularly potent in curing the plague. People wore or carried it as a charm that looked something like this:

```
A B R A C A D A B R A
A B R A C A D A B R
A B R A C A D A B
A B R A C A D A
A B R A C A D
A B R A C A
A B R A C
A B R A
A B R
A B
A
```

It was believed that the sickness would fade away as the words on the paper slowly faded.

Many people followed doctor's orders and took medicine to prevent contracting the plague. Here is one recipe:

"Take five cups of [the herb] rue if it be a man, and if it be a woman leave out the rue, for rue is a restorative to a man and wasting to a woman; and then take thereto five crops of [the herb] tansey and five little blades of [the flower] columbine, and a great quantity of marigold flowers full of the small chives from the crops that are like saffron chives. And if you may not get the flowers, take the leaves, and then you must have of the marigolds more than the others. Then take an egg that is newly laid, and make a hole in either end, and blow out all that is within. And lay it to the fire and let it roast 'til it may be ground to powder, but do not burn it. Then take a quantity of good treacle [a medicinal syrup], and bray all these herbs therein with good ale, but do not strain them. And then make the sick drink it for three evenings and three mornings. If they hold it, they shall have life."

This prayer was used to ward off the plague. It presents an interesting combination of belief in God and in astrology:

"Star of Heaven, who nourished the Lord and rooted up the plague of death which our first parents planted; may that star now deign to counter the constellations whose strife brings the people the ulcers of a terrible death. O glorious star of the sea, save us from this plague. Hear us: for your son who honours you denies you nothing. Jesus, save us, for whom the Virgin Mother prays to you."

## THE REACTION OF THE PEOPLE

Many people took matters into their own hands rather than consulting a doctor. Boccaccio mentions that some people isolated themselves, living "sober and abstemious" lives. Yet in the next breath he describes how others did the exact opposite, choosing to "enjoy life to the full, go round singing and merry-making, gratify all of one's cravings whenever the opportunity offered, and shrug the whole thing off as one enormous joke."

Throughout the plague, people were in constant fear for their lives and witnessed horrific death daily. They may be excused for resorting to excessive measures in an attempt to understand and prevent the plague from overtaking them. Jean de Venette describes an extreme religious movement that arose at the height of the epidemic:

"Men in Germany, Flanders, Hainaut, and Lorraine uprose and began a new sect on their own authority. Stripped to the waist, they gathered in large groups and bands and marched in

**Flagellants beat themselves in hope that God would spare them from the plague.**

procession through the crossroads and squares of cities and good towns. There they formed circles and beat upon their backs with weighted scourges, rejoicing as they did so in loud voices and singing hymns suitable to their rite and newly composed for it. . . . They flogged their shoulders and arms with scourges tipped with iron points so zealously as to draw blood."

De Venette adds that this religious sect, known as the Flagellants, was later denounced by Pope Clement as having been "damnably formed." De Venette expressed his own contempt for the movement by saying "their many errors showed how little they knew of the Catholic faith."

Not all people turned on themselves. Many sought to blame others as the cause of the plague. Women were targeted in some areas, especially those thought to have loose morals. Minority groups became instantly suspect. Lepers—people who suffered from the disease leprosy—were often scapegoats, as were Muslims. Pilgrims from other countries were regarded with suspicion, too. But the prime suspects were the Jews.

Jews and Christians had long been at odds. Christians were intolerant of the Jews because they refused to accept Jesus. That Jews were believed to have crucified Jesus was enough reason for many Christians to hate them. Another was the fact that Jews were the primary moneylenders during the Middle Ages. The Catholic

Burning in a pit: falsely accused of having spread the plague, Jews became targets of persecution and violence.

Church forbade loaning money for interest; however, many Christians had borrowed money from Jews before the plague. It is human nature to resent those to whom we are indebted. This resentment, combined with centuries of anti-Semitism, made many Christians only too willing to believe whatever rumors they heard about the Jews.

Many rumors about Jews were spread by members of the clergy. These rumors alleged that Jews routinely kidnapped and tortured Christian children; that they consorted with the devil; that they sought to murder Christians by poisoning their meat and wine. With such a foundation of hatred firmly planted in Christian minds, it was simple enough to blame the plague on the Jews.

Jews were thought to have spread the plague by poisoning the drinking water in Christian communities. Transcripts of confessions from several Jews survive; they seemed to offer the proof needed to point the finger at the Jewish community. On the heels of such confessions—undoubtedly gotten through torture or force—came officially encouraged massacres, or pogroms, of Jews.

The persecution originated in Germany. Heinrich Truchess von Diessenhoven, a former chaplain, left this account of the pogroms taking place in his area:

"First Jews were killed or burnt in Solden in November, then in Zofingen they were seized and some put on the wheel [a form of torture], then in Stuttgart they were all burnt. The same thing happened during November in Landsberg . . . and in Bueron, Memmingen and Burgau. . . . During December they were burnt and killed on the feast of St. Nicholas in Lindau, on 8 December in Reutlingen, on 13 December in Haigerloch, and on 20 December in Horw they were burnt in a pit. . . . Once started, the burning of the Jews went on increasing."

Although Pope Clement VI prohibited the killing of Jews in 1348, pointing out that Jews were dying of the plague just as readily as Christians, the persecution didn't end until late 1349. Jewish communities had all but vanished by then. It would take fifteen years for them to recover.

Of course, persecuting and killing Jews didn't stop the plague. And in the end, all the confessions, medical advice, folk remedies, talismans, and prayers were worthless. Wherever the plague struck, it was unstoppable.

# CHAPTER FIVE

# PICKING UP THE
## ~ PIECES ~

*In the face of so much affliction and misery, all respect for the laws of God*
*and man had virtually broken down and been extinguished. . . .*
*Hence everyone was free to behave as he pleased.*

—Boccaccio, The Decameron

Y 1351 THE WORST OF THE PLAGUE WAS OVER.
Yet its effects were just beginning to be felt. No part
of life would, or in fact could, ever be the same.

Imagine what it must have been like to have lived while all
those around you died a horrible death. On the one hand, survivors felt boundless relief at having been spared. Death had
stared them in the faces, and they hadn't succumbed.

On the other hand, what the survivors had seen, heard,
and smelled during the months of death was forever burned
into their memories. In addition, countless numbers of their
friends, family, and acquaintances were gone. It would have
been impossible for them to simply pick up their lives again.
So how did they think and behave once the crisis was over?

*Opposite:*
In this nightmarish
scene of the plague
years, painted by Jan
Brueghel in the
sixteenth century,
Death (in the form of
a skeleton) triumphs
over all.

## SURVIVORS' PSYCHOLOGY

Florentine chronicler Matteo Villani made the following observation:

"It was thought that the people . . . having seen the extermination of their neighbors and of all the nations of the world . . . would become better, humble, virtuous and catholic, avoiding iniquities and sins and overflowing with love and charity for one another. . . . The opposite happened. Men, finding themselves few and rich by inheritances and successions of earthly things, forgetting the past as if it never was, gave themselves to the most disordered and sordid behavior than ever before."

In short, people were living in the moment and thinking of their own satisfaction. They didn't care if their behavior was immoral or even criminal. Death had robbed them of friends and relatives yesterday; who knew if it would come back for them today or tomorrow?

In the past such an individualistic attitude was not the norm. People were brought up to work for the collective good of the family, the manor, the monastery, or the guild, not for themselves. But these communities were devastated during the plague years. Even the family unit had fallen apart. The plague had taught people the bitter lesson that the only one you could count on was yourself and, therefore, you were the only person you owed anything to. Pessimism replaced the optimistic attitude that had begun to emerge prior to the Black Death.

Hand in hand with this pessimism was an obsession with pain and death. This obsession was reflected in the art created during the years immediately following the plague. Images of death adorned murals, paintings, frescoes, and tombstones.

This style of artwork is known as the *danse macabre*, the Dance of Death. It included dancing skeletons tormenting humans, a shadowy, scythe-carrying figure named the Grim Reaper stalking unsuspecting victims, and worm-ridden corpses rotting alongside the living.

Religious artwork changed dramatically as well. Before the plague, the images were generally bright, lighthearted, and welcoming. Mary and Jesus were bathed in a holy glow. After the Black Death, Mary and Jesus were shown as much more somber and distant.

A portrait of Laura, Petrarch's lost love

Literature spent a greater number of pages dwelling on death. Sometimes such musings were thoughtful, recollecting the loss of a loved one to the plague. This excerpt from a poem by Petrarch, an Italian diplomat and poet who survived the plague but lost his beloved Laura, is one such example:

> Great is my envy of death whose curt hard sword
> Carried her whom I called my life away;
> Me he disdains, and mocks me from her eyes!

Other works of literature, such as an anonymous poem entitled "It Is Good to Think on Death," in which a dead woman debates the loss of her beauty with the worms who are consuming her, focus on the inevitability of death. Still others, such as this passage by Eustace Deschamps, a fourteenth-century French poet, express feelings of futility:

"Happy is he who has no children, for babies mean nothing but crying and stench; they give only trouble and anxiety; they have to be clothed, shod and fed; they are always in danger of falling and hurting themselves; they contract some illness and die. When they grow up, they may go bad and be put in prison. Nothing but cares and sorrows; no happiness compensates us for our anxiety, for the trouble and expense of their education."

Most survivors sorted out their feelings about death subconsciously. They had more important things to deal with, chief among them being the simple matter of making a living.

## DEPOPULATION

Before the plague, there were plenty of people to do the work necessary to keep things operating smoothly. Then suddenly, one-third of the work force was gone—and with it a way of life that had existed for centuries.

Before the plague, landlords had more than enough people to work their land. After the plague, just the opposite was true. Suddenly, finding people to tend a lord's fields was no easy task.

The labor shortage gave members of the peasant class some new advantages. A passage from William Langland's work *Piers Ploughman* sums up the situation:

"The beggars refused the bread that had beans in it, demanding milk loaves and fine white wheaten bread. And they would not drink cheap beer at any price, but only the best brown ale that is sold in the towns.

"And the day labourers, who have no land to live on but their shovels, would not deign to eat yesterday's vegetables. And draught-ale was not good enough for them, nor a hunk of bacon, but they must have fresh meat or fish, fried or baked. . . .

"And so it is nowadays—the labourer is angry unless he gets high wages, and curses the day that he was ever born a workman."

In the plague's wake, peasants demanded higher wages for their work.

For the first time, the free peasant could pick and choose where he wanted to work. He could demand higher wages, as much as double what he had earned prior to the plague. If he didn't get them from one lord, he could find another who was eager to pay. In addition to wages, many peasants insisted on receiving other benefits, such as the gift of a cow, or a better plow, or even fresh meat instead of the salted kind.

Landlords had little choice but to give in to these demands or else lose their workers. They tried to control the movement of laborers by passing laws prohibiting peasants from leaving one manor for another. Other laws attempted to put a cap on wages. But they were to no avail. The peasants saw their opportunity and rose to take it.

*On the next page:* Finding laborers to perform the many tasks of farming and animal husbandry became difficult.

However, whatever advantages most peasants gained were short-lived. For even as rents decreased and labor shortages drove up the fees for services, the cost for many types of food and goods increased. Any gains the peasant class might have made with increased wages were typically canceled out by higher costs.

Landlords also felt the pinch of rising costs. To make matters worse, most couldn't farm the same expanse of land they had before the plague. There just weren't enough field hands to do the work. At the same time, the value of land and the price of certain crops had decreased. Faced with this dismal economic situation, the lords needed to figure out something new to do with their land.

Many landholders switched from farming to animal husbandry. Raising sheep and cattle was much less labor-intensive than cultivating crops. Animal husbandry was also more profitable than farming because wool, mutton, milk, and beef were hard to come by.

Some lords let their less fertile fields return to forests. Other landholders leased plots of land to former serfs. These peasants now had the wherewithal to get rich off the land, just as their former masters had done.

However, some peasants discovered that there were easier ways of getting rich. All around them were the homes and belongings of dead people—rich and poor. When no one came forward to claim these things, peasants took them for their own. Suddenly, once unattainable housing and luxury items were readily available.

Peasants also flocked to the cities, where some were accepted into the artisan guilds. Guilds had been in existence for generations. Master craftsmen ran the guilds and controlled

all aspects of the manufacture and trade of their wares and services. To become a master craftsman, one had to train for years, passing through the ranks of apprentice and journeyman before presenting a final masterpiece and achieving the rank of master.

Before the plague, guilds mainly accepted apprentices whose fathers, brothers, or uncles were already members. When the plague struck, guilds lost craftsmen of all ranks. In order to regain their numbers, many guilds were forced to open their doors to people with no previous connection.

During the postplague years, guilds often hurried apprentices through their training, bestowing upon them the rank of master long before they were truly accomplished at their craft. The result was an era of sub-par goods and poor services.

Those peasants who were accepted usually found themselves better off financially than they were before. Some made the jump from lower to middle class.

As the people in the lower class built up wealth, they began to live better. With money, they could buy finer clothes, food, and shelter. This did not sit well with the members of the upper class, who felt that such outward signs of class mobility were presumptuous. The nobles set out to put a stop to it.

In England, they passed a set of rules known as sumptuary laws. These laws were put forth in an effort to preserve class distinctions. For example, only nobles were allowed to wear the best furs as full-length garments. Merchants and others of the middle class could wear fur, but only as trim. Those of the lowest birth were not allowed to wear any fur at all. That way, one could tell at a glance who belonged to which class.

But the lords were not in a position to enforce these laws. In fact, with the deaths of so many of them, the nobility had

**A wealthy lady in fine clothes is followed by her more modestly dressed servant.**

lost its strong hold on the law. Peasants fought back against the attempts to suppress their upward mobility.

Pockets of revolt sprang up in the decades that followed the Black Death. Some were relatively insignificant, not much more than looting and pillaging. But others, such as the Peasants' Revolt in England in 1381, had a greater impact. Facing a mass of infuriated peasants, King Richard II, then still a teenager, promised freedom from serfdom to all who asked for it. He also promised to put an end to a number of taxes and laws designed to suppress the peasant class—promises he later broke.

## THE CHURCH

Another slice of the population hit hard by the plague was the clergy. Monasteries were swept nearly clean. Villages and towns were left without priests and bishops. In short, the Church had a serious labor shortage. If it was to regain its power over the people, it needed to fill the vacancies as quickly as possible.

It accomplished this by lowering its standards or overlooking previously hard-and-fast rules. Middle-aged men widowed by the plague—and in a few cases, even men whose wives were still alive—were ordained as priests. Younger men than usual were ushered into the fold and quickly given responsibilities for which they were not ready. Some priests accepted multiple benefices, church appointments that included a wage and living quarters, which meant they had to divide their time among several parishes. Others were promoted to higher stations before they were truly ready to do all that was required of them. In extreme cases, women were allowed to perform the sacred rituals.

The Church's influence would never be quite as strong as it had been before the Black Death. Throughout the plague years, medieval people had turned to the Church for answers, for comfort, and for the rituals that eased them into and through life and into death. But the Church failed them on many levels.

First of all, the Church failed when it couldn't stop the plague by correctly interpreting God's wishes. If God was angry with humankind, what did humankind have to do to appease Him? It was only too clear that the Church didn't know. No matter what people did in the name of God, the plague just marched on. God wasn't listening.

The Church had also abandoned its flock in a very real way. While some clergymen rose to the occasion, sacrificing their own safety to continue performing their duties, countless others reacted to the plague in an all-too-human fashion. Some fled in the face of danger. Others stayed, but demanded payment in exchange for their presence at a plague victim's bedside or funeral—something strictly forbidden by the Church—and even flaunted their new wealth in public. Still others broke the vow of chastity they had taken when they joined the Church.

Most people found the flight of priests during the Black Death shameful. These verses illustrate their reproach:

> You pope-holy priests, full of presumption
> With your wide furred hoods void of discretion

Unto your own preaching of contrary condition
Which causes the people to have less devotion.

After the plague ended, many people turned their backs on the Church they felt had abandoned them. Some took matters of religion into their own hands. An Englishman named John Wycliffe translated the Bible from Latin into English. When the printing press came into use, his Bible made the word of God accessible to more people. Many historians believe the seeds of the Protestant Reformation—a religious movement in the early sixteenth century that was based on the concept that people could commune directly

John Wycliffe reads from his translated Bible.

THE BLACK DEATH

with God without the need of priests—were planted in the postplague years.

Not all people abandoned their faith. Some reinforced it by dedicating their lives, land, and money to doing good works in the hopes of achieving salvation. Hospitals, which in the Middle Ages cared for the poor and provided shelter for the sick, were often beneficiaries of such a person's charity. After the plague, donations to hospitals rose by 50 percent in some areas, and new hospitals were created through generous endowments. Money to finish or begin building cathedrals or to bolster churches poured in. Bequests in wills funded the pilgrimages of many people to religious shrines. These tangible expressions of faith may have been made with the selfish aim of securing one's place in heaven, but their effect on the society as a whole was nothing but selfless.

## REPOPULATION

When the Black Death had finally run its course, it was up to the survivors to literally repopulate Europe. According to Jean de Venette, many did just that:

"When the epidemic was over the men and women still alive married each other. Everywhere women conceived more readily than usual. None proved barren, on the contrary, there were pregnant women wherever you looked. Several gave birth to twins, and some to living triplets."

Not all marriages were made for the sake of reproduction, however. Many a man's fortune was made when he married a rich girl orphaned by the plague. William Langland, author of *Piers Ploughman*, wrote that such marriages "for greed of goods and against natural feeling" left

It was hoped that weddings such as this one would lead to children.

mismatched couples with "guilt and grief." He asserted that these marriages were childless, too, further making his point that such unions were no good. The town of Siena was also against these unions. It passed a law that forbade any heiress from marrying without the consent of a kinsman.

It would take Europe until the 1500s to reach its pre-plague population. Urban areas recovered sooner than rural ones, mostly because people migrated from the country to the city in search of wealth, jobs, and other people. Once settled, they married and gave birth to a new generation.

THE BLACK DEATH

## CHANGES IN LEARNING

Universities had been in existence in Europe for more than two centuries before the plague. However, they were few and far between; no more than thirty such institutions were in operation at the time of the plague. Of these thirty, five were forced to close when the plague robbed them of students and professors.

Yet, in the years immediately after the plague, the number of universities increased significantly. Some were funded through religious bequests, while others came into being in response to a need for highly educated clerics. Others grew out of a fear of travel spawned by the plague—those seeking a higher education no longer wished to journey far, and so local universities were opened.

Teachers for these new universities were often brought up from lower schools because they had a working understanding of Latin, the language of higher education.

That left openings in the grammar schools. These were filled by less educated people, people who had little working knowledge of Latin. So instead of teaching in Latin, these educators used their own languages, known as the vernacular. Boys graduated from grammar school and continued on to college unable to understand or speak much Latin. Those who had been taught some Latin rarely used a pure form of the ancient language. Rather, they spoke and wrote a medieval version.

This situation was intolerable to many universities. In Italy a movement grew to restore the Latin language to its original state. The movement spread to other universities in other countries. Yet, at the same time, the use of the vernacular continued to grow in lower schools.

The use of different languages ultimately increased the intellectualism of the era after the plague. Those schooled in

Latin preserved knowledge available only in that language—texts of ancient Greek and Roman thinkers such as Aristotle and Plato—while those who learned in their native tongues were the beneficiaries of an education they might not have had otherwise. The better educated a society is, the more likely it is to grow culturally. Many historians believe the dual progress of Latin and the vernacular led to the Renaissance, the era of cultural rebirth that occurred from the mid-fourteenth century through the sixteenth.

## THE PLAGUE AND PUBLIC HEALTH

Most cities had been completely caught off guard when the plague hit. Those that had boards of health found them sorely lacking during the plague years. The Black Death should have served as a wake-up call for the need of a system of safeguarding the health of the public. But it took several recurrences of the plague before most towns and cities began to heed the call. It wasn't until the seventeenth century that boards of health were created in many cities. They tried to address the problems

A Dutch house in the seventeenth century. The broom and the dog and cat show that cleanliness and rodent control were becoming important to people.

believed to have helped cause and spread the plague. They also began to supervise the practices of physicians and to report and isolate any case of the plague or other contagious disease.

Art, literature, economics, education, religion—these were just a few of the areas that underwent change in the aftermath of the plague. In truth, no European was untouched. From the highest-born noble to the lowliest peasant, every person alive before, during, or, if they were lucky, after the Black Death was changed somehow—financially, emotionally, socially, or otherwise. And though other changes were centuries in the future, the Black Death marks a dividing line between what was and what was to be.

ercie upon us †

# *The* SURVIVAL OF
# ~ *Y. PESTIS* ~

HE PLAGUE RETURNED TO EUROPE in epidemic proportions a mere twelve years after the Black Death ended. It lasted for about a year. The death rate was about 10 to 20 percent of a population still trying to recover from the first epidemic. Seven years later it struck again, claiming an estimated 10 percent of the population.

In fact, for the next four hundred years, the plague would stalk humankind. Cairo lost 300,000 people in the fifteenth century. In 1665 *Y. pestis* devastated London, killing an estimated 68,000 out of 1 million people before the Great Fire of 1666 laid waste to the rat population and its breeding places. Marseilles, France, fell victim in 1720–1721. This was the last

*Opposite:* The plague gripped London in its deadly hands once again in 1665.

55

The Diseases and Casualties this Week.

London 35   From the 15 of August to the 22   1665

A page from a London almanac lists the diseases and deaths that occurred during the week of August 15–22, 1665. In one week, 3,880 Londoners died of plague.

major outbreak of plague in western Europe. The ports of China were struck in 1894, the same year that Alexandre Yersin and Shibasaburo Kitasato discovered the *Y. pestis* bacterium.

Yet even after the discovery, the plague still roams the earth. The United States is not immune. The Centers for Disease Control (CDC) in Atlanta, Georgia, reports between ten and fifteen cases annually. Rats are not always the carriers of the diseased fleas in these cases. Coyotes, bobcats, squirrels, rabbits, and even household cats and dogs have been the culprits. Sometimes the infected person had come into contact with the dead animal's carcass, and the fleas jumped from the dead to the living. Other times, close contact with a live but infected animal led to human infection.

Bubonic plague is usually curable through immediate

treatment with heavy doses of antibiotics. Yet the most likely areas for plague outbreaks are either poverty-stricken third-world countries, where rats and humans live side by side, or sparsely populated rural sites where contact with wildlife is frequent. Medical facilities with the necessary drugs are often difficult to reach from such places, if they are available at all.

Even so, it's unlikely that the world will ever experience a plague epidemic on the scale of the Black Death again. The World Health Organization (WHO) has an ongoing program aimed at wiping out the plague. And the CDC can mobilize a treatment team to combat and contain any outbreaks. Still, new and deadly diseases attack every day. We can only hope for and work toward cures for the Ebola virus, AIDS, and other killers before they claim one-third of our population.

# TIME LINE OF THE BLACK DEATH

**1320–1346**

The Black Death ravages China and the Middle East

**1347**

The Black Death reaches the Crimea, including Kaffa

**October 1347**

The Black Death enters the port of Messina, Sicily, via trade ships from the East

**Fall/Winter 1347**

Sicily is overwhelmed

**January 1348**

The Black Death enters France through the port of Marseilles; northern Italy is struck down

**February 1348**

Population of Avignon, France, is cut in half by the plague

**April 1348**

The Black Death reaches the interior of Italy

**Spring 1348**

Massacres of Jews begin

**May 1348**

The Black Death strikes Paris

**June 1348**

The Black Death continues to spread across Europe, crossing the Alps into Bavaria

**July 1348**

Normandy is struck

**August 1348**

The Black Death enters England through the port of Bristol

**September 1348**

London succumbs to the Black Death; Pope Clement VI issues a papal bull calling for the end of pogroms against Jews

**End of 1348**

The Black Death fades away in Italy

**March 1349**

The Black Death continues to spread through England and into Ireland

**May 1349**

Scandinavia is struck

**Summer 1349**

The Black Death strikes Tournai in Flanders (now Belgium)

**July 1349**

Scotland succumbs

**December 1349**

Pogroms against the Jews finally stop in Germany, but continue elsewhere

**Early 1350**

The Black Death spreads throughout the Netherlands

**Spring 1350**

Eastern Europe is struck

**1351**

The Black Death vanishes from Europe, only to return twelve years later

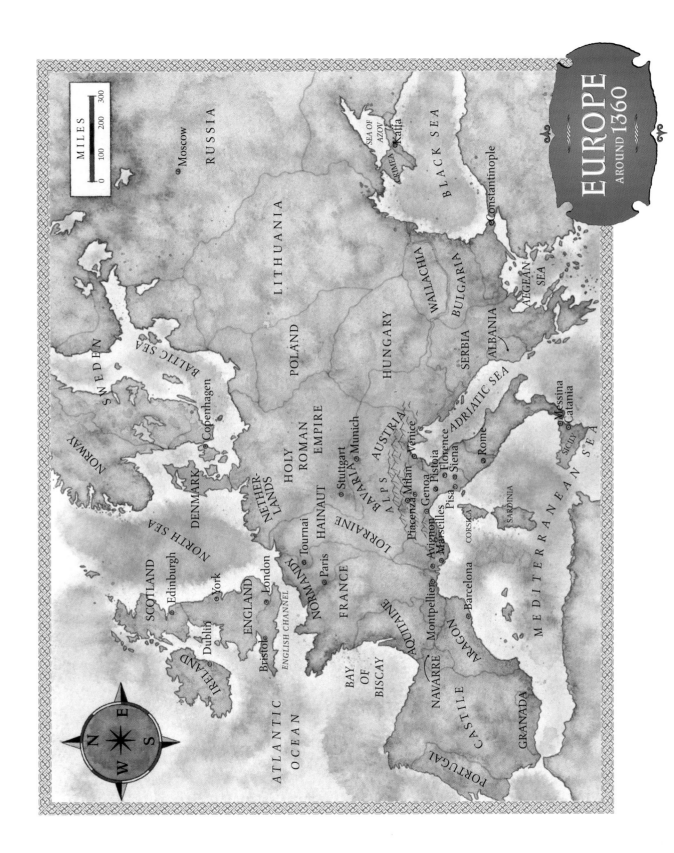

EUROPE
AROUND 1360

MILES
0  100  200  300

RUSSIA

Moscow

LITHUANIA

POLAND

SWEDEN

BALTIC SEA

NORWAY

DENMARK

Copenhagen

NETHER-
LANDS

HOLY
ROMAN
EMPIRE

HAINAUT

HUNGARY

WALLACHIA

BULGARIA

SERBIA

ALBANIA

BLACK SEA

SEA OF
AZOV

CRIMEA
Kaffa

Constantinople

AEGEAN
SEA

ADRIATIC SEA

AUSTRIA

Munich
Stuttgart

BAVARIA

ALPS

Milan
Placenza

Genoa

Venice
Pistoia
Florence
Siena

Pisa

Rome

Messina
SICILY
Catania

SARDINIA

CORSICA

MEDITERRANEAN  SEA

LORRAINE

NORTH SEA

SCOTLAND

Edinburgh

York

ENGLAND

London

Bristol

ENGLISH CHANNEL

IRELAND

Dublin

NORMANDY

Tournai

Paris

FRANCE

AQUITAINE

BAY
OF
BISCAY

Montpellier

Avignon
Marseilles

Barcelona

ARAGON

NAVARRE

CASTILE

PORTUGAL

GRANADA

ATLANTIC
OCEAN

N
E
S
W

59

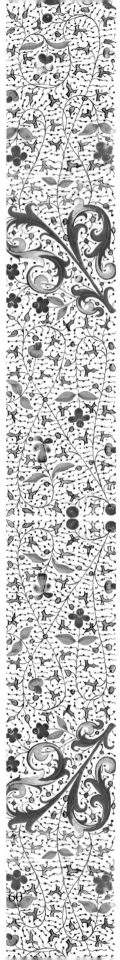

## GLOSSARY

**abbot** the head of a monastery for men

**agrarian** pertaining to the cultivation of land; agriculture

**artisan** a person who works as an artist or craftsperson

**buboes** pus-filled egg-sized swellings of the lymph glands of the neck, armpits, and groin; typically found in cases of bubonic plague

**chastity** the state of being virtuous or celibate

**chronicle** a written narrative of an event or events

**chronicler** a person who writes a narrative of an event or events

**Crimea** a peninsula that juts from the southern part of Ukraine into the Black Sea and the Sea of Azov; the Crimea may be said to be a crossroads between East and West, since it lies in the region where the continents of Europe and Asia meet

**Crusades** wars fought between Christians and Muslims in the eleventh, twelfth, and thirteenth centuries

***danse macabre*** artwork and literature that portray Death dancing among the unsuspecting living

**delirium** a confused state of mind often brought on by serious sickness and fever

**galley** a large, shallow ship propelled by oars and sails that was used for war or to carry cargo

**guild** a professional association of craftspeople or merchants united by their trade

**heriot** a payment owed to the lord of the manor by a serf's family upon the serf's death; usually the family's best animal, such as a cow or horse

**hierarchy** a system of rank according to ability or status

**manorialism** a self-sustaining system of land management, economics, and society in Europe during the Middle Ages. Nobles owned land worked on by peasants, who owed the nobles labor and payments in exchange for housing, protection, and land to till.

**miasma** a poisonous cloud believed to spread disease to all who come into contact with it

**monastery** a community of religious persons, usually monks, who live together; also, the place where they live

**parish** a subdivision of a diocese that is ministered to by a priest or other religious figure

**sumptuary laws** laws passed in the late 1300s aimed at maintaining class distinctions by prohibiting lower classes from dressing as if they belonged to higher classes

**urbanization** general movement away from country life to city life

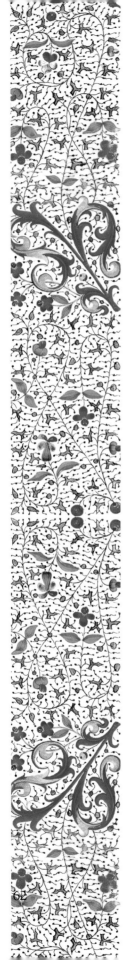

## TO FIND OUT MORE

### BOOKS

Altman, Linda Jacobs. *Plague and Pestilence: A History of Infectious Disease*. Springfield, NJ: Enslow Books, 1998.
A well-written overview of a variety of diseases, including a section on the Black Death.

Archer, Jules. *Epidemic! The Story of the Disease Detectives*. New York: Harcourt Brace Jovanovich, 1977.
An interesting look at the role of the epidemiologist in uncovering the cause of infectious disease. Includes a chapter on recent cases of the bubonic plague.

Biel, Timothy Levi. *The Black Death*. San Diego: Lucent Books, 1989.
A good overview of the disease, aimed at younger readers.

Corzine, Phyllis. *The Black Death*. San Diego: Lucent Books, 1997.
An informative look at the disease and the Middle Ages, written for middle-grade readers. Includes black-and-white illustrations, maps, and contemporary source material.

Dunn, John M. *Life During the Black Death*. San Diego: Lucent Books, 2000.
Presents a clear picture of what life was like before, during, and after the Black Death, written for middle-grade readers. Includes black-and-white illustrations and contemporary source material.

Hinds, Kathryn. *Medieval England* (Cultures of the Past series). New York: Marshall Cavendish, 2001.
A cleanly written history of England during the Middle Ages; includes a good chapter on the different social classes.

Oleksy, Walter. *The Black Plague*. New York: Franklin Watts, 1982. Written for younger readers; offers a fairly detailed look at the plague and the Middle Ages.

**ON THE INTERNET\***

"Bubonic Plague" at
http://www.ponderosa-pine.uoregon.edu/students/Janis/menu.html
A fascinating question-and-answer tour of the Black Death, including pictures.

"The Bubonic Plague" at
http://www.mrdowling.com/703-plague.html
A straightforward account of the Black Death; includes a map detailing the spread of the disease.

"The Black Death" at
http://www.insecta-inspecta.com/fleas/bdeath/Black.html
Created by students, this site offers basic information on the plague along with some interesting pictures.

"The Plague in Europe" at
http://members.tripod.com/eurohist/main.html
Historical overview of the plague with some interesting pictures.

"The History of the Black Death" at
http://www.geocities.com/julia09/blackdeath
A well-organized site about life before, during, and after the plague.

\*Websites change from time to time. For additional on-line information, check with the media specialist at your local library.

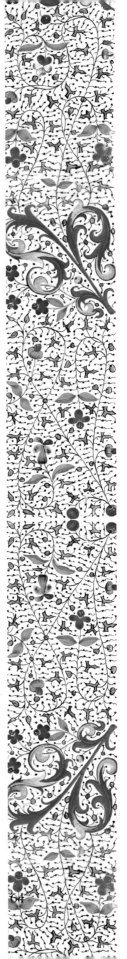

## BIBLIOGRAPHY

Archer, Jules. *Epidemic! The Story of the Disease Detectives.* New York: Harcourt Brace Jovanovich, 1977.

Biel, Timothy Levi. *The Black Death.* San Diego: Lucent Books, 1989.

Boccaccio, Giovanni. *The Decameron.* Translated by G. H. McWilliam. New York: Penguin Books, 1972.

Bowsky, William M., ed. *The Black Death: A Turning Point in History?* New York: Holt, Rinehart & Winston, 1971.

Bray, R. S. *Armies of Pestilence.* New York: Barnes and Noble Books, 1996.

Cantor, Norman. *In the Wake of the Plague: The Black Death and the World It Made.* New York: The Free Press, 2001.

———*The Civilization of the Middle Ages.* New York: HarperCollins, 1993.

Cohen, Daniel. *The Black Death: 1347–1351.* New York: Franklin Watts, 1974.

Corzine, Phyllis. *The Black Death.* San Diego: Lucent Books, 1997.

Dunn, John M. *Life During the Black Death.* San Diego: Lucent Books, 2000.

Gottfried, Robert S. *The Black Death: Natural and Human Disaster in Medieval Europe.* New York: The Free Press, 1983.

Herlihy, David. *The Black Death and the Transformation of the West.* Cambridge, MA: Harvard University Press, 1997.

Herlihy, David, ed. *Medieval Culture and Society.* New York: Harper & Row, 1968.

Horrox, Rosemary, trans. and ed. *The Black Death* (Manchester Medieval Sources series). Manchester: Manchester University Press, 1994.

Marks, Geoffrey. *The Medieval Plague: The Black Death of the Middle Ages*. Garden City, NY: Doubleday, 1971.

McKay, John P., Bennett D. Hill, and John Buckler. *A History of Western Society*. 3rd ed. Vol. 1. Boston: Houghton Mifflin Company, 1987.

Nardo, Don, ed. *The Black Death* (Turning Points in World History series). San Diego: Greenhaven Press, 1999.

Oleksy, Walter. *The Black Plague*. New York: Franklin Watts, 1982.

Siraisi, Nancy G. *Medieval and Early Renaissance Medicine*. Chicago: University of Chicago Press, 1990.

Southern, R. W. *The Making of the Middle Ages*. New Haven: Yale University Press, 1970.

Tuchman, Barbara W. *A Distant Mirror*. New York: Alfred A. Knopf, 1978.

Ziegler, Philip. *The Black Death*. New York: Harper & Row, 1969.

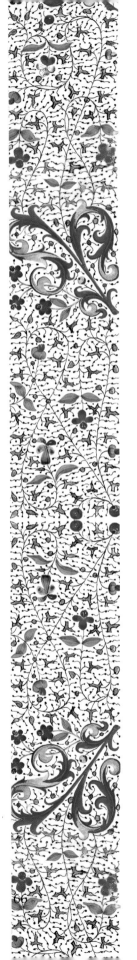

## NOTES ON QUOTATIONS

The quotations in this book are from the following sources:

**Chapter One: The Plague Comes to Europe**

p. 1: "In October 1347," Horrox, *The Black Death*, p. 36.

p. 3: "People suffer," Ibid., p. 42.

p. 5: "Civilization both in," Dunn, *Life During the Black Death*, p. 27.

p. 6: "They ordered corpses," Horrox, *The Black Death*, p. 17.

p. 7: "Alas," Ibid., p. 19.

**Chapter Two: Europe before the Plague**

p. 8: "The one who was," Herlihy, *The Black Death and the Transformation of the West*, p. 32.

**Chapter Three: Eyewitnesses to Death**

p. 18: "How many gallant," Boccaccio, *The Decameron*, p. 58.

p. 19: "This scourge," Ibid., p. 54.

p. 19: "Being confined," Ibid., p. 56.

p. 20: "Members of a household," Bowsky, *The Black Death: A Turning Point in History?*, p. 13.

p. 21: "And it was all," Ibid., p. 14.

p. 22: "over one hundred thousand," Boccaccio, *The Decameron*, p. 57.

p. 23: "So high was," Ibid., p. 16.

p. 24: "The sick are," Horrox, *The Black Death*, p. 44.

p. 24: "Every day the bodies," Ibid., pp. 51—52.

p. 24: "Thoughtful men," Ibid., p. 61.

p. 25: "in 1348," Ibid., p. 62.

p. 25: "The pestilence held," Ibid., p. 69.

p. 25: "I, seeing these," Ibid., p. 84.

p. 26: "With such a disaster," Ibid., p. 81.

**Chapter Four: Where Did It Come From?**

p. 27: "[God said]," Horrox, *The Black Death*, p. 15.

p. 33: "Take five cups," Dunn, *Life During the Black Death*, p. 60; "Star of Heaven," Horrox, *The Black Death*, p. 124.

p. 34: "sober and abstemious" and "enjoy life," Boccaccio, *The Decameron*, p. 52.

p. 34: "Men in Germany," Bowsky, *The Black Death: A Turning Point in History?*, p. 17.

p. 35: "damnably formed" and "their many errors," Ibid., p. 18.

p. 36: "First Jews," Horrox, *The Black Death*, p. 208.

**Chapter 5: Picking up the Pieces**

p. 38: "In the face," Boccaccio, *The Decameron*, pp. 52–53.

p. 40: "It was thought," Herlihy, *The Black Death and the Transformation of the West*, p. 65.

p. 41: "Great is my envy," Dunn, *Life During the Black Death*, p. 73.

p. 41: "Happy is he," Gottfried, *The Black Death: Natural and Human Disaster in Medieval Europe*, p. 89.

p. 42: "The beggars refused," Corzine, *The Black Death*, p. 85.

p. 47: "You pope-holy," Gottfried, *The Black Death: Natural and Human Disaster in Medieval Europe*, p. 84.

p. 49: "When the epidemic," Horrox, *The Black Death*, p. 57.

p. 49: "for greed of goods" Tuchman, *A Distant Mirror*, p. 117.

p. 50: "guilt and grief," Ibid., p.117.

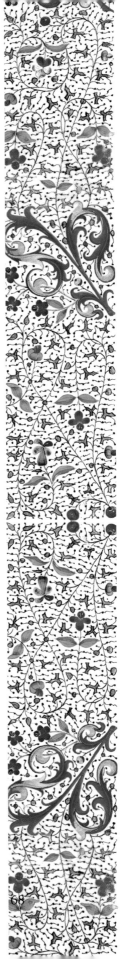

# INDEX

**Page numbers for illustrations are in boldface**

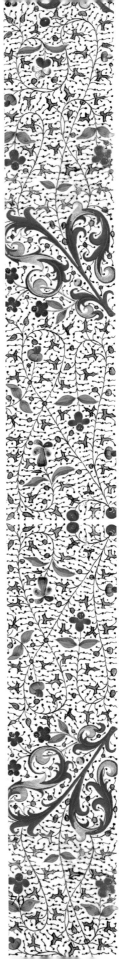

## ABOUT THE AUTHOR

STEPHANIE TRUE PETERS grew up in Westborough, Massachusetts. After graduating with a degree in history from Bates College, she moved to Boston where she worked as an editor of children's books. She made the jump from editor to writer soon after the birth of her son. Since then, she has authored a number of nonfiction books for young people, including the other titles in the Epidemic! series. Stephanie lives in Mansfield, Massachusetts, with her husband, Dan, and their two children, Jackson and Chloe. She enjoys going on adventures with her family, beachcombing on Cape Cod, and teaching kick-boxing classes at the local YMCA.

## DATE DUE

| | | | |
|---|---|---|---|
| JA 1 0 06 | | | |
| FEB 08 | | | |
| MAR 17 | | | |
| MAR 31 | | | |
| DE 4 | | | |
| | | | |
| | | | |
| | | | |
| | | | |
| | | | |
| | | | |
| | | | |
| | | | |
| | | | |
| | | | |
| | | | |
| | | | |

DEMCO 38-296